MIRACLES

WALT WHITMAN'S BEAUTIFUL CELEBRATION OF LIFE

Illustrated by
Jim Hamil   Fred Klemushin   David R. Miles   Jim Paul

♛ *Hallmark Crown Editions*

MIRACLES

WHY,
WHO MAKES MUCH
OF A MIRACLE?

AS TO ME, I KNOW OF NOTHING ELSE BUT MIRACLES...

...WHETHER I WALK THE STREETS OF MANHATTAN...

OR DART MY SIGHT
OVER THE ROOFS
OF HOUSES
TOWARD THE SKY...

OR WADE
WITH NAKED FEET
ALONG THE BEACH
JUST IN THE EDGE
OF THE WATER...

OR STAND UNDER TREES IN THE WOODS...

OR TALK BY DAY

WITH ANY ONE
I LOVE...

OR SLEEP
IN THE BED

AT NIGHT
WITH ANY ONE
I LOVE...

OR SIT AT
THE TABLE
AT DINNER
     WITH THE REST...

OR LOOK
AT STRANGERS
OPPOSITE ME
RIDING
IN THE CAR...

OR WATCH
HONEY-BEES BUSY
AROUND THE HIVE
OF A SUMMER
FORENOON...

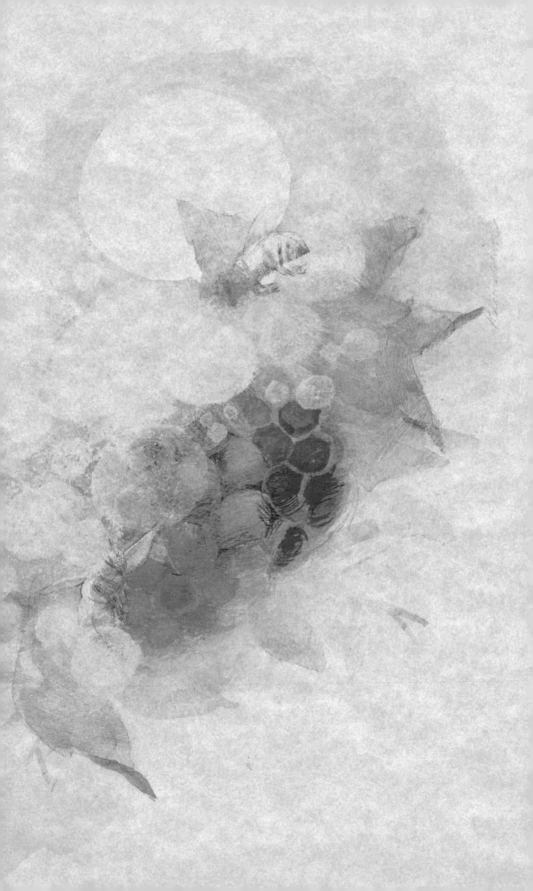

OR ANIMALS
FEEDING
IN THE FIELDS...

OR BIRDS...

OR THE WONDERFULNESS OF INSECTS IN THE AIR...

OR THE WONDERFULNESS OF THE SUNDOWN...

OR OF STARS...
SHINING SO QUIET
AND BRIGHT...

OR THE EXQUISITE
DELICATE
THIN CURVE
OF THE NEW MOON
IN SPRING...

THESE
WITH THE REST,
ONE AND ALL,
ARE TO ME
MIRACLES...

THE WHOLE
REFERRING...
YET EACH DISTINCT
AND IN ITS PLACE.

TO ME EVERY HOUR OF THE LIGHT...

EVERY CUBIC INCH OF SPACE

IS A
MIRACLE...

EVERY
SQUARE YARD
OF THE
SURFACE
OF THE
EARTH
IS SPREAD
WITH THE SAME...

EVERY FOOT
OF THE
INTERIOR
SWARMS
WITH
THE SAME.

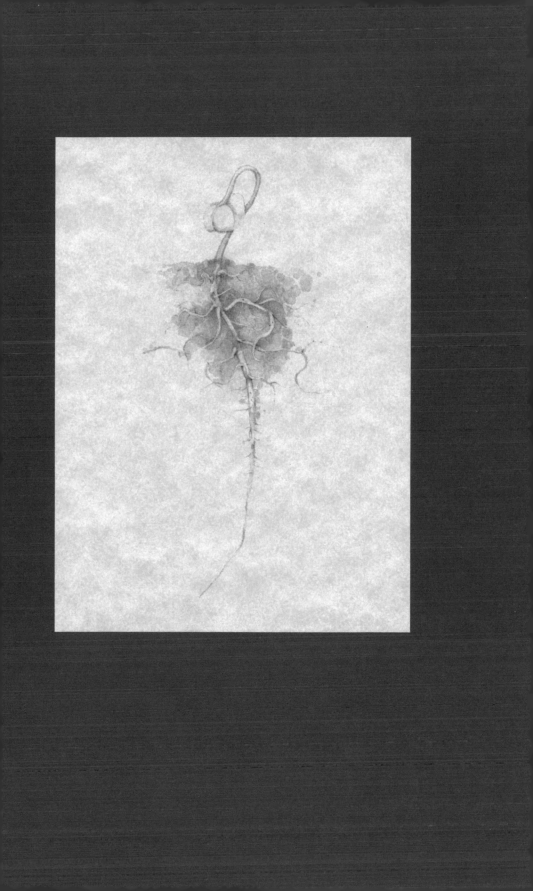

TO ME
THE SEA
IS A CONTINUAL
  MIRACLE...
THE FISHES
THAT SWIM...
THE ROCKS...

THE MOTION OF THE WAVES... THE SHIPS WITH MEN IN THEM...

WHAT STRANGER MIRACLES ARE THERE?

This book was designed by David R. Miles.
The typeface is Torino, an English design from an
Italian foundry.
The paper is Hallclear, White Imitation Parchment
and Ivory Fiesta Parchment.
The cover is bound with book cloth and Torino paper.